THIS JOURNAL
belongs to

LEARN, GROW, SUCCEED!

A KID'S GROWTH MINDSET JOURNAL

LEARN GROW SUCCEED!

BRANDY THOMPSON

ILLUSTRATIONS BY ALYSSA NASSNER

ROCKRIDGE
PRESS

Interior and Cover Designer: Merideth Harte
Art Producer: Sara Feinstein
Editor: Susan Randol
Production Editor: Andrew Yackira
Illustrations: Alyssa Nassner
Illustrations © 2019 Alyssa Nassner
Author photo courtesy of © Kelly Day Portraits (Germantown, TN).

ISBN: Print 978-1-64152-626-5
Printed in Canada

This book is dedicated
to the loving memory of
my mom, Nancy Garrison
Richardson. I will forever
admire her strength
and courage. Her words
of encouragement still
empower me to this day.

Welcome to Your Journal!

What if I told you that everything you need to be successful in life is already inside you?

You have the power within you to learn, grow, and succeed. This journal is going to help you discover this ability through something called *growth mindset*.

It all starts with your brain.

Did you know that your brain can grow and change, like the muscles in your body?

This is good news! It means that you decide how much success you want to have. You get to choose your future. With the right attitude, you can do great things. Sometimes, though, unhelpful thoughts can get in your way. This journal is going to help you get rid of those thoughts. You will learn how to change your thinking and become confident, brave, and happy. It does not matter who you are or where you come from. Everything you need to be successful is inside you, waiting for you to tap into it.

What Is Growth Mindset?

Growth mindset is the belief that your mind "grows." Hard work is the answer to getting stronger, faster, and better. The opposite of a growth mindset is a fixed mindset. This is the belief that people are born a certain way and that they are stuck like that.

Here are two examples of the difference between a fixed mindset and a growth mindset:

Fixed: "I'm not an athlete."
Growth: "I can get better at sports if I practice."
Fixed: "I can't do this."
Growth: "I can do hard things if I keep trying new ways to do them."

As you write in this journal, you'll want to keep in mind these eight basic growth mindset beliefs:

1. Effort and hard work are the key to success, not just talent.
2. Mistakes and failures help you learn.
3. Unhelpful thoughts limit you.
4. You can create positive thoughts.
5. Frustration is a normal part of growth.
6. Comparison can hold you back.
7. Feedback and criticism are important for change.
8. Change is good.

Adapting a growth mindset has lots of benefits. With a growth mindset, you will:

- believe in yourself and your abilities.
- be proud of your effort, not just your grades.
- not worry anymore about mistakes and failures.
- bravely try new things.
- replace unhelpful thoughts with positive thoughts.
- love new challenges.
- accept change.
- not let pride or passing feelings stand in your way.
- stop comparing yourself to others.
- be free to become **your best self**.

How to Use This Journal

This journal is for you to use the way that you want to use it. You can start on any page and choose how often you work in it. There's no right or wrong way to do it. Just pick a page and follow the directions. Have fun being creative and adding your own doodles, drawings, and thoughts!

Think about these helpful tips before you start using your journal:

- Create a comfy spot just for journaling. Find a place where you can relax and let your thoughts flow. Maybe you have a favorite spot near a window or a cozy chair that you love. Play music that relaxes you, and grab a stuffed animal or fidget toy.

- Don't judge yourself and don't judge anything you put in the journal. Write down your first thoughts without worrying about perfection. No one is going to grade you on your spelling or grammar, so let loose and be yourself.

- Always keep the journal in the same place so it's easy to find when you want it. Give it a home where you can see it every day as a reminder to use it.

- When you read one of the quotes that are scattered throughout the journal, take a minute to think about what it means. Quotes aren't always easy to understand the first time you read them. It may take a few times before you get what the author is really saying to you. Try to find the author's lesson or advice in the quote.

This journal offers thought-provoking prompts and quotes. When you're finished, read the "Not the End" section in the back of the book to reflect on your favorite ways to master growth mindset. I hope that you'll keep the journal for a very long time and continue to look at it when you need to be reminded how to learn, grow, and succeed.

I'm so happy you have chosen to go on this journey! I'm excited for you to discover higher self-esteem, less worry, and greater success because of your new way of thinking.

MISTAKES ARE HELPFUL

Everybody makes mistakes. Famous people, your teachers, and even the leaders of countries make mistakes. You will, too. It's normal. You decide how to react when you make a mistake. You can get upset or find the lesson in it.

What lesson would you learn if you lost your homework because you weren't organized?

_____

_____

_____

What would you do differently to make sure it didn't happen again?

_____

_____

What could you say to someone else who made a mistake?

_____

_____

_____

Describe a time when you were proud of yourself. How did your body feel?

_____

_____

_____

_____

_____

Changing your idea of what makes you proud will help you deal with mistakes. Instead of being proud of a grade, be proud of the work you did to get it. List three times when you worked hard to get something.

_____

_____

_____

_____

_____

_____

_____

It can be tempting to blame others for your mistakes, but it's better (for you and others) to admit them. Write about a time when you were brave enough to tell the truth about a mistake you made. How did you feel?

_____

_____

_____

_____

_____

_____

How do you act when other people make mistakes? Do you treat them the way you would want other people to treat you?

_____

_____

_____

_____

_____

Mistakes are gifts when they teach us a lesson. Write a mistake you made in each of the gift boxes. Below each one, tell about the lesson (gift) you learned from it.

_____

_____

_____

_____

Change your thinking from "I made a mistake when . . ." to "I learned a lesson when . . ." Try it now.

I learned a lesson when . . .

_____

_____

_____

_____

_____

Use Positive Self-Talk

The words you say to yourself matter. You will begin to believe the things you think, so make sure your thoughts are good ones. Repeat these positive words to yourself out loud as you trace the letters.

I am strong.
I learn from my mistakes.
I am proud of my effort.

List three more positive chants to say to yourself.

_____

_____

_____

List three things that you do well.

_____

_____

_____

Keep your mind focused on happy thoughts. What are some of your favorite things?

Movie: _____

Book: _____

Song: _____

Game: _____

Memory: _____

Joke: _____

Now finish these sentences:

I am thankful for _____

_____.

One thing I wouldn't want to do without is _____

_____.

I love it when _____

_____.

"Keep your face to
the sunshine and you
cannot see a shadow."

—Helen Keller, American political activist

When you are filled with happy thoughts, your brain has less room for negative thoughts.

Pretend that when you wake up tomorrow, you will have magical powers and can do anything you want. Describe your perfect day. No limits!

_____

_____

_____

_____

_____

_____

_____

_____

_____

_____

_____

_____

_____

_____

What thoughts have you had about yourself lately (both good and bad)? If they are mean thoughts, write them on the spiderweb to feed to the spider. If they are nice thoughts, write them on the flowers.

Now try it again without the web. This time, ignore your negative thoughts. Write down the three best thoughts you have about yourself. Try this every time you think about yourself. Ignoring mean thoughts gets easier with practice.

_____

_____

_____

LEARN TO LOVE FEEDBACK

How do you feel when someone points out your faults or mistakes?

_____

_____

_____

_____

_____

_____

Think of a time when someone told you that you messed up. How did you feel? Why did you feel that way?

_____

_____

_____

_____

_____

_____

Feedback can be helpful, but not all feedback is good. You need to decide if the feedback you receive will help you fix your mistake. Try it now.

What mistake did you make?

_____

_____

_____

_____

_____

What feedback did you receive? Was it helpful?

_____

_____

_____

_____

Can you fix your mistake using the feedback? How?

_____

_____

_____

_____

It's normal to get upset when someone points out that you messed up. But remember that everybody makes mistakes, so you don't have to feel bad. Practice being nice to the people who show you your faults.

What's something nice you could say to someone who pointed out a mistake you made?

_____

_____

_____

_____

_____

_____

Finish this sentence:

I don't have to get upset when somebody tells me

I messed up because _____

_____

_____

_____

_____.

Being humble is important if you want to learn from feedback. (It's also a good way to make more friends. People like humble, happy people.)

How can you be humble?

- Don't brag or talk about yourself too much.
- Let others have their turn.
- Admit mistakes.
- Don't take all the credit.
- Be happy for others, too.
- Be able to laugh at your mistakes.

Can you remember a time when you weren't humble and didn't react well to feedback? How would you react to that feedback now?

_____

_____

_____

_____

_____

_____

_____

_____

_____

FOCUS ON THINGS YOU CAN CONTROL

weather

other people's thoughts

divorce

Don't waste time worrying about things you can't control. Work on the things you can control. The big cloud lists things you cannot control. The small cloud lists things you can control. Add at least three things to each cloud.

my thoughts

my words

my actions

Give an example of you being in control of your words, thoughts, or actions.

_____

_____

"Don't let what
you cannot do
interfere with what
you can do."

—John Wooden, former UCLA basketball coach

Pack a suitcase with worries.

In the suitcase, write three things that are out of your control that worried you today or this week.

Imagine closing the suitcase and putting those worries out of your mind.

How could you control the following situations?

When my brother yells, I can _____

_____

_____.

When someone is mean to me, I can _____

_____.

When you worry, use one or more of the ideas on this list. Once you tame your worries, you can focus on the things you can control.

- ☐ **Close your eyes and count to 20.**
- ☐ **Exercise or take a walk outside.**
- ☐ **Squeeze a stress ball then slowly let it go.**
- ☐ **Complete a puzzle or maze.**
- ☐ **Draw, write, or do a craft.**
- ☐ **Hang out with a pet.**

List three more things that you would enjoy.

_____

_____

_____

Name three people you can talk to when you worry.

_____

_____

_____

Your job is to be a kid! Let adults worry about the big stuff. What do kids tend to worry about? Schoolwork, what to wear, and how to make friends. These are all things you can control.

List a kid-size worry.

_____

_____

_____

_____

_____

What can you do to get rid of this worry?

_____

_____

_____

_____

_____

_____

DON'T LET FRUSTRATION GET YOU DOWN

Challenges help you grow and change, but they can be frustrating. Learning to deal with frustration leads to success.

How does your body feel when you're frustrated?

_____

_____

_____

_____

_____

How do you calm down when you're frustrated?

_____

_____

_____

_____

_____

_____

"All successful people learn that success is buried on the other side of frustration."

—Tony Robbins, life coach

Here's what to *say* to yourself when you're frustrated:

- Everyone gets frustrated.
- This is normal.
- Frustration helps me learn and grow.
- It will pass.

How have you dealt with frustration in the past?

_____

_____

_____

What could you say to yourself the next time you're frustrated?

_____

_____

_____

What would you say to a friend who is frustrated?

_____

_____

_____

Here's what to *do* when you're frustrated:

- Take a break.
- Get a snack.
- Start over.
- Use words to describe your feelings.
- Look for new ways to solve your problem.
- Ask for help.

What is your favorite way to relax and take a break?

_____

_____

_____

_____

_____

List three people who can help you when you're frustrated.

_____

_____

_____

Keep your eyes on the prize! Remembering your goal helps you overcome frustration.

Challenge: You have to speak to the class about a book you haven't read.

Another thing I can do to prepare

One thing I can do to prepare

How will you feel when your speech is over?

_____

_____

_____

SETTING GOALS PUTS YOU IN CHARGE

If you don't plan where you're going, you might end up where you don't want to be.

What is something important that you hope to do by the time you are grown?

_____

_____

_____

What goals could you set for yourself to make it happen?

_____

_____

_____

Draw a picture of yourself as an adult reaching this goal.

"A goal without a plan is just a wish."

—Antoine de Saint-Exupéry, French writer

Long-term goals are things you want to do, or accomplish, in more than a year from now.

What do you want to accomplish next year?

_____

_____

_____

_____

What do you want to accomplish in five years?

_____

_____

_____

_____

What do you want to accomplish in ten years?

_____

_____

_____

_____

Short-term goals are things that you want to achieve in a shorter period of time. These often help you get to your long-term goals.

List one of your long-term goals.

_____

Come up with three short-term goals that will help you achieve this long-term goal.

Next week:

_____

_____

_____

Next month:

_____

_____

_____

Next year:

_____

_____

_____

Don't let obstacles stop you from reaching your goals. Not having enough money or time are a couple of things that could stop you or slow you down from reaching your goals. When you come to an obstacle, you need to find a way around it.

List some obstacles you have come across before that didn't stop you.

_____

_____

_____

_____

_____

Who helped you get through them?

_____

_____

_____

_____

_____

Flex Your Brain to Think Big

You can have confidence in your ability to do things because your brain "grows" when you learn. Just like working the muscles in your body, you can train your brain.

List some things that used to be really hard for you to do but are now easy.

_____

_____

_____

Draw a picture of you trying something for the first time.

Now write about how it feels to try that thing again after a lot of practice.

_____

_____

"Attitude is a little thing that makes a big difference."

—Winston Churchill, British prime minister

Your attitude about your brain's ability helps you succeed, so don't waste time doubting yourself. Be confident and go for it.

Think of a time you were convinced you couldn't do something, but you did it. What was it you thought you couldn't do?

_____

_____

_____

_____

Did adopting a positive attitude help? If so, how? If not, what would you tell yourself, now that you know a positive attitude helps you succeed?

_____

_____

_____

_____

_____

_____

_____

Your stretchy brain has room to keep growing your whole life. There are no limits, so think big!

What is something that you would learn if you had unlimited time to practice?

_____

_____

_____

When something seems too big or scary, the hardest part of getting started is the first step. What is a first step you could take to begin learning this skill?

_____

_____

_____

_____

What are some other steps you could take?

_____

_____

_____

_____

Imagine that you are an adult writing a book about your life. You had great success because you weren't afraid to think big and go for your dreams.

What would you name the book?

_____

Complete the first page of your book.

_____

_____

_____

_____

_____

_____

_____

_____

_____

_____

ATTITUDE OF GRATITUDE

Gratitude, or a feeling of thanks, can spark the positive attitude you will need when working on a growth mindset. Take a minute at the end of each day to reflect on the things that improve your life.

I am thankful for these three things (or people) that I can see right now.

When I close my eyes, I am thankful for these three things.

I will be thankful for these three things that I hope to have one day.

The Earth provides us with many gifts such as food, water, and animals. What are some things you are thankful for that the Earth gives you?

_____

_____

_____

_____

_____

_____

Sometimes you can say thank you by helping someone or something. You can help the Earth by watering plants and recycling. What is something else you could do for the Earth?

_____

_____

_____

_____

_____

_____

Think about the people who make your life better. They could be family members, friends, or anyone you know.

Someone I'm thankful for: _____

This is one of my favorite memories with them: _____

_____

_____

Here's what I could do or say to thank them: _____

_____

_____

Someone else I'm thankful for: _____

This is one of my favorite memories with them: _____

_____

_____

Here's what I could do or say to thank them: _____

_____

_____

You can be thankful for almost anything. Complete this gratitude scavenger hunt. You may need to hunt for facts.
I am thankful for:

a moment in history that made life better: _____

_____

_____

an invention that makes life easier: _____

_____

_____

a rule that keeps me safe: _____

_____

_____

a group of people that keep me safe: _____

_____

_____

DON'T GET CAUGHT IN THOUGHT!

Your brain is wired to have automatic thoughts. Keep the helpful thoughts and ignore the negative thoughts that cause self-doubt.

Helpful: "I can do this. I'll try my best."
Unhelpful: "I'm not good at tests. This is too hard."

Don't say things to yourself that you wouldn't say to a good friend. What would you say to a friend before a big test?

_____

_____

_____

Draw a picture of yourself feeling positive before a test.

Change your focus from *perfection* to *improvement*.

When you try to be perfect, you set yourself up for failure.

Instead of "I need to make all A's," think "I want to improve my grades from last time."

Now you try it!

Instead of "My handwriting must be perfect," think "_____

_____."

Instead of "My art has to be perfect," think "_____

_____."

Copy this three times: "I am proud of progress, not perfection."

_____

_____

_____

_____

_____

_____

"Don't worry about failures, worry about the chances you miss when you don't even try."

—Jack Canfield, American writer

Another thought trap is believing you know what others are thinking by the way they're acting. But when you guess, you often guess wrong. If you catch yourself trying to guess a friend's thoughts, stop and ask them what they're thinking.

Write about a time when you made a wrong guess about what someone was thinking.

_____

_____

_____

What made you believe you knew what they were thinking?

_____

_____

_____

What could you do the next time you start to guess why a friend is acting a certain way?

_____

_____

_____

Don't get caught up in stewing over things. Do you sometimes think, "I wish I had done something else instead," or "Why did I do that?" If you're sitting around worrying, you're wasting your time.

What is something you have worried about too much?

_____

_____

_____

_____

Did sitting and thinking about it change anything?

_____

_____

_____

What is something you could do about it instead of worrying about it?

_____

_____

_____

_____

COMPARISON AND COMPETITION

Everyone is unique. There will be times when you'll be able to do something really well while your friends struggle. At other times, you'll struggle with something that others find easy.

List three things that are really easy for you.

_____

_____

_____

What comes easily for your friends that may be more of a struggle for you?

_____

_____

_____

Explain why this is okay.

_____

_____

_____

"When the game is over I just want to look at myself in the mirror, win or lose, and know I gave it everything I had."

—Joe Montana, former football player

Comparing yourself to others is not helpful. You should only compare yourself to you. Look for improvement in yourself.

List three things you have improved in your life.

_____

_____

_____

List three things you would like to improve even more.

_____

_____

_____

What could you say to someone who wants to compare grades with you?

_____

_____

_____

_____

_____

_____

Become the best version of *you*. Competitions can be fun, but that's all they should be. Don't get too upset when you don't win. Nobody else is just like you, so comparing yourself to others is never a fair comparison.

What is something unique about you?

_____

_____

_____

_____

What competitions do you enjoy?

_____

_____

_____

_____

Why do you like them?

_____

_____

_____

_____

You are in charge of a new competition. In this competition you're competing with yourself, not others. Maybe you'll win the award for a better attitude!

What are some other improvement awards you hope to win? Write them on the prizes below.

Write an acceptance speech for one of those awards.

Award: _____

Speech: _____

_____

_____

_____

TOO MUCH GRIT TO QUIT

Grit is having a good attitude and trying again, even when a task seems too hard.

Look at these parts of GRIT:

G: Good attitude

R: Ready to try new things when I fail

I: I won't quit

T: Trust myself to do it

Complete these sentences:

I had a good attitude when _____

_____.

I tried something new when _____

_____.

I wanted to quit but I didn't when _____

_____.

I trust myself because _____

_____.

Look back at the elements of *grit*. How could you "stick it out" if the following things happened?

You lost a puzzle piece.

_____

_____

_____

_____

You got the wrong answer on a math problem.

_____

_____

_____

_____

You're reading a difficult book.

_____

_____

_____

_____

"Anything's
possible if you've
got enough nerve."

—J. K. Rowling, British writer

Grit requires trust. You need to trust *yourself*.

Do you trust yourself to do hard things? Why? Or why not?

_____

_____

_____

_____

_____

_____

Write about a time when you thought you couldn't do something, but you did it anyway.

_____

_____

_____

_____

_____

How did that feel?

_____

_____

Quitting is easy. Being able to get back up and try again is harder. Do you have the *grit* to keep trying?

I didn't quit when _____

_____

_____

_____

_____

_____

_____

_____ .

When I feel like quitting, I can _____

_____

_____

_____

_____

_____

_____

_____ .

Challenge Yourself

A challenge is something new that takes a lot of effort or *grit*. Some challenges will come to you, but you can also create your own challenges to become your best self.

How can you challenge yourself this week to become a better person?

_____

_____

_____

What will you need to do to prepare for this challenge?

_____

_____

_____

What can you say to yourself when the challenge becomes difficult?

_____

_____

_____

Try a healthy habits challenge! Think about your eating habits, your physical activity, and how you treat yourself. List one or two habits that you could improve.

_____

_____

Create a challenge for yourself that would help you improve these habits. Be realistic, but make sure it's not too easy. What is your challenge and when will you complete it?

Challenge: _____

_____

_____

_____

_____

_____

_____

Completion date: _____

Try a school challenge! Think about your study and work habits and ways you could improve them.

List a few things that you could do better.

_____

_____

_____

Create a challenge for yourself that would help you improve these habits. What is your challenge and when will it be completed?

Challenge: _____

_____

_____

_____

_____

_____

_____

_____

Completion date: _____

Try a partner challenge! Having someone to support you can make a challenge more successful and fun. Every day, report your progress to a partner.

Friend's name: _____

What is your challenge? _____
_____

Day 1 / We will _____
_____.

Day 2 / We will _____
_____.

Day 3 / We will _____
_____.

What did you learn from your partner challenge?

_____
_____
_____
_____

CHALLENGES BRING GOOD CHANGES

Bigger challenges bring bigger change. And learning
to love bigger challenges will help you grow even faster.
What big challenge can you start now?

_____

_____

How would this challenge help you grow?

_____

_____

What was the biggest challenge you've ever faced?

_____

_____

What lesson did you learn from it?

_____

_____

"The roughest roads often lead to the top."

–Christina Aguilera, pop singer

The only way to take on a big challenge is one step at a time. For example, if you were asked to clean the entire house, you would start with one room, then clean another room, and so on.

Look at the stair steps. On each step, write smaller actions you could take to complete the challenge listed on the wall.

ORGANIZE
YOUR
BACKPACK

Change how you see challenges. Create a positive way to reframe fixed mindset statements. Here's an example:

FIXED

I have to do 10 difficult math problems.

Growth

I am learning so many math strategies.

Now it's your turn!

FIXED

Our coach makes us practice so much.

Growth

FIXED

My teacher
is making
us clean
our desks.

Growth

FIXED

I have to read
a whole book
this weekend.

Growth

Now that you know how to think positively about *your* challenges, you can help others reframe *their* challenges. Write positive things you could say to people in these situations.

A younger student is angry because she can't figure out how to complete a puzzle.

_____

_____

_____

Your cousin is crying because she has to clean the very messy kitchen.

_____

_____

_____

A classmate looks worried about the new project your teacher assigned.

_____

_____

_____

BE AWESOME WITHOUT
NEEDING APPROVAL

No matter how hard you try, you can never make everyone like you. When you get too worried about what others think, you forget what really matters.

What are some things in your life that matter the most?

_____

_____

_____

_____

_____

Are these things more important than what others think about you? Why? Or why not?

_____

_____

_____

_____

_____

Knowing your strengths is like having a shield that protects you from mean things other people may say.

List your strengths in the shield, then write about your strengths on the lines that follow.

I know that I am good enough because _____

_____

_____.

I am _____

_____

and nobody can take that away from me.

Sometimes people do things they don't want to do just to make others happy. Write about a time when you did something you didn't want to do and why you did it (this doesn't include chores or homework!).

_____

_____

_____

_____

Why is it hard to say no sometimes?

_____

_____

_____

_____

How do you feel when somebody tells you no?

_____

_____

_____

_____

Instead of "How will this make me look," think "How will this help me grow?"

How much time do you spend thinking about what others think about you?

_____

_____

Why do you care what they think?

_____

_____

Does their opinion help you grow or change who you are?

_____

_____

_____

What can you say to somebody who doesn't seem to like you?

_____

_____

_____

STOMP OUT FEAR

Fear often gets in the way of success. Try challenging a fear. Most of the time, the fear isn't that big a deal once you face it.

I am not afraid of _____

_____ anymore.

List three reasons why you're not afraid of it anymore.

_____

_____

_____

Draw yourself stomping out this fear.

"Being brave isn't the absence of fear. Being brave is having that fear but finding a way through it."

—Bear Grylls, survival instructor

You are braver than you think.

List three times when you had to be brave. (For example, did you ever get a cast on a broken bone, sleep in the dark, or sing on stage?)

_____

_____

_____

Who helped you during those times?

_____

_____

_____

_____

What did you say or do to make yourself feel better?

_____

_____

_____

_____

Pretend you have zero fear. Complete these sentences:

If I knew I would not fail, I would _____

_____

_____

_____

_____.

If I believed I could do anything, I would _____

_____

_____

_____

_____.

If I could erase one fear, it would be the fear of _____

_____

_____

_____

_____.

Unplug the power of fear. You can take the power away from a fear by:

- learning facts about it.
- trying to conquer the fear a little bit at a time instead of all at once.

For example, if you were afraid of swimming, you could:

- find out facts about swimming.
- go near the water the first time and get in the water the second time.

Name a fear you have. _____

_____

List three facts about it.

_____

_____

_____

Write two small steps you could take before trying to conquer your entire fear.

_____

_____

THE BEST IS YET TO COME

One word can change everything. Add *yet* to show you have a growth mindset.

Instead of "I cannot swim," say "I cannot swim **yet**. If I practice three times I week, I can do it."

This shows that you are willing to do the work.

I cannot _____ yet.

If I _____, I can do it.

I cannot _____ yet.

If I _____, I can do it.

I cannot _____ yet.

If I _____, I can do it.

I cannot _____ yet.

If I _____, I can do it.

I cannot _____ yet.

If I _____, I can do it.

There are many things you can do, and some that you cannot do, yet. You are always growing and getting better. Think about your past. Fill in the spaces with things you could and could not do at different ages.

Baby

I could do this: _____

I could not do this yet: _____

Age 5

I could do this: _____

I could not do this yet: _____

Now

I can do this: _____

I can't do this yet: _____

List three things you can do really well.

_____

_____

_____

Create a list of things you cannot do yet but hope to do someday.

_____

_____

_____

Make a list of things you will need to practice to make your list of goals come true.

_____

_____

_____

In the first box, draw a picture of someone trying to do a difficult task.

In the second box, write about or draw a picture of the things they need to do to learn the skill.

In the third box, draw a picture of them mastering the skill.

"It's not that I'm so smart, it's just that I stay with problems longer."

—Albert Einstein, German physicist

What Gets You Going?

With a growth mindset, you are motivated by growth. Motivation is the reason behind why you do something. You do things for three main reasons:

- For the joy of it (you are happy to learn or grow; you enjoy it).
- To get a reward (you want better grades).
- To avoid punishment (you don't want to be yelled at or grounded).

Always aim to be motivated by growth.

Write about a time you did something because you were motivated by the joy of doing it.

_____

_____

_____

_____

How did it feel?

_____

_____

_____

Motivation can come from others.

Write about a time when you did something just so you wouldn't get in trouble.

_____

_____

_____

_____

Write about a time when you did something for a reward (such as a toy or money).

_____

_____

_____

_____

Do you think you would keep doing those things if you didn't get the reward? Why? Or why not?

_____

_____

_____

_____

Motivation can come from inside you.
List three things you do just for the joy of it.

_____

_____

_____

List three things you do because you feel like it's "the
right thing to do."

_____

_____

_____

How does your attitude or mood affect your motivation
to do things?

_____

_____

_____

_____

_____

_____

_____

What makes you want to work hard? With a growth mindset, growth is your goal, not your reward. If you are stuck thinking that learning is forced on you, you might expect a reward. Stay focused on how the learning you do today helps your future.

If you had never learned anything before today, how would your life be different?

_____

_____

_____

_____

_____

What are some other things you want to learn so that you will have a good future?

_____

_____

_____

_____

_____

_____

NOBODY'S PERFECT, AND THAT'S OKAY!

Many wonderful things aren't perfect. Roses have thorns but they are still beautiful.

Think of somebody you really like. List three things about them you really like.

_____

_____

_____

List three things about them that show they aren't perfect.

_____

_____

_____

Explain why you still like them.

_____

_____

_____

"If you look for perfection, you'll never be content."

–Leo Tolstoy, Russian writer

Write a paragraph about a perfect world where everyone is the best at everything, nobody has to work to get anything, and everyone likes all the same things.

_____

_____

_____

_____

_____

What do you not like about that world?

_____

_____

_____

_____

What would make it better?

_____

_____

_____

_____

Change your mindset from wanting *perfection* to wanting *progress* or growth.

Find the good or growth, no matter how small.

For example: I fell off my skateboard. At least I'm getting better at skating on it.

I don't run as fast as my friends. At least _____

_____

_____.

Our team didn't win. At least _____

_____

_____.

I didn't _____

_____

_____.

At least _____

_____

_____

_____

_____.

It's okay to laugh at yourself instead of crying when you mess up. Try adding "and that's okay" when you talk about your faults.

Here's an example: I write my numbers backward, and that's okay.

I _____ and that's okay.

I _____ and that's okay.

I _____ and that's okay.

I _____ and that's okay.

How do you feel when you laugh at the mistakes you make instead of getting angry?

_____

_____

_____

_____

_____

_____

_____

_____

SELF-RESPECT MAKES YOU STRONGER

Self-respect means loving yourself exactly the way you are now. Be proud of the things you do, instead of being proud of how you look or what awards you win.

List three things you have done that make you proud.

_____

_____

_____

What compliment could you give to someone about their actions instead of their looks?

_____

_____

_____

What compliments have you been given about your actions?

_____

_____

_____

_____

A rainbow has many colors, just like you have many qualities that make you special. Write something good about yourself on each band of the rainbow.

This makes me unique: _____

People say I am good at: _____

This is my best talent: _____

Having respect for yourself means that you set rules for how you want to be treated—for example, "Don't make fun of me." You also respect others by following their rules.

Keep in mind, though, that sometimes rules are unfair and shouldn't be followed (for example, "I always go first").

List five rules for how you want to be treated.

_____

_____

_____

_____

_____

Write about a time when your rules were broken.

_____

_____

_____

Draw how you felt when this happened.

If friends keep breaking your rules, tell them how you feel. If they still don't quit, find new friends.

Fill in the blanks with things you could say to friends who break your rules.

When you talk mean to me, I feel _____

_____

_____

_____

_____.

When you lie to me, I feel _____

_____

_____

_____.

When you _____, I feel

_____

_____

_____

_____.

FINDING YOUR JOY

What are some things that get you excited? Describe how your body feels when you are doing something you really love.

_____

_____

_____

_____

_____

What is something you could do every day for a year and never get tired of it?

_____

_____

_____

_____

_____

"The two most important days in your life are the day you are born and the day you find out why."

—Mark Twain, American writer

Fear of the unknown might stop you from trying things that may bring you joy. But the more you try new things, the easier trying new things becomes. If you knew you could not fail, list the things you would try.

A sport: _____

_____

A club or group: _____

_____

A musical instrument: _____

_____

Imagine yourself doing one of these things successfully. Draw yourself happily trying it.

There may be something you haven't tried yet that could bring great joy to your life.

Look at the "Try Tree." List things on the leaves that you still want to try.

People I can ask to try new things with me:

_____

_____

_____

Set a deadline. Choose an activity that you are afraid to try. Make a time frame for when you want to try it.

I want to try _____

by _____.

People I can ask for help with this: _____

_____

_____

I want to try _____

by _____.

People I can ask for help with this: _____

_____

_____

I want to try _____

by _____.

People I can ask for help with this: _____

_____

_____

SHOW ME THE GROWTH

Let's look at how you are growing and changing. You have the power to set goals and make real changes in your life. You can get rid of unhealthy habits and start new healthy habits.

List three new habits you want to start.

_____

_____

_____

Draw a picture of yourself doing some of these things.

How would your life be different if you were doing these things more often?

_____

_____

_____

"No matter how good you get, you can always get better, and that's the exciting part."

–Tiger Woods, pro golfer

Sometimes old habits get in the way of your growth. List four habits (for example, chewing pencils) that are not helping you become a better student.

_____

_____

_____

_____

It takes about a month to train your mind and body to change an old behavior, so don't get upset if it doesn't happen right away.

What are some healthy habits that could replace these bad habits? For example, you would say, "Instead of chewing school supplies, I could chew gum."

Instead of _____,

I could _____.

Instead of _____,

I could _____.

Instead of _____,

I could _____.

Name a subject in school that you want to do better in. Think about how you can do more to understand this subject.

List the steps you can take to learn more and do better.

_____

_____

_____

_____

If one of your steps includes study time, when will you study?

_____

_____

Your grade now: _____

What do you want your next grade to be after you make

the changes? _____

List some things that you already do well. Do you need to keep getting better at them? If you have a growth mindset, your answer was yes. There's always room to grow.

Make some growth goals.

I can _____ well.

I will _____

more so that I can get better at it.

I can _____ well.

I will _____

more so that I can get better at it.

I can _____ well.

I will _____

more so that I can get better at it.

Differences Make You Awesome

Everybody has bones and skin. Everybody breathes and has feelings.

List three other things about the body that are the same for everyone.

_____

_____

_____

List three things that everyone does the same.

_____

_____

_____

Write about some things that make you different from most people.

_____

_____

_____

"We all live with the objective of being happy; Our lives are all different and yet the same."

–Anne Frank, German-born diarist

Celebrate differences, especially differences between you and your friends.

What is something you like that your friend doesn't like?

_____

What is a talent you have that your friend doesn't have?

_____

Where have you been that your friend hasn't been?

_____

What is something your friend likes that you don't like?

_____

What is a talent your friend has that you don't have?

_____

Where has your friend been that you haven't been?

_____

How do these things make your friendship more fun or exciting?

_____

You can learn many things from people who are different from you. If you only talk to people who are just like you, you won't be able to grow as much. Challenge yourself to always include others.

List three people who are very different from you who you aren't friends with yet.

_____

_____

_____

Talk to one of them and learn three facts about them.

_____

_____

_____

List three things you have in common with them.

_____

_____

_____

Nobody can do everything really well. You may be good at some things but not as good at other things. Pretend you are on a secret mission and need people with special talents to help. List people you would hire who are the best at:

reading _____

math _____

running _____

singing _____

cooking _____

drawing _____

writing _____

COMMUNICATING
WITH OTHERS

Your mindset is important when you speak to others, especially during a disagreement. With a fixed mindset, you may get stuck on hurt feelings and shut down. With a growth mindset, you look for the lesson and grow from it.

What emotions do you feel when somebody disagrees with you?

_____

_____

Draw what your face looks like.

How does the look on your face affect how the other person reacts to you?

_____

_____

Sometimes you will have to compromise or give up part of what you want so that everyone can win a little. You might have to share or take turns.

How could you compromise in the following situations?

You and your friend want to watch different movies.

_____

_____

_____

_____

Your little brother is crying because he wants your seat.

_____

_____

_____

_____

You and your friend both want the last cookie.

_____

_____

_____

_____

Using "I feel" statements helps take some of the blame off the other person and keeps an argument positive. For example, instead of "You yelled and made me upset," say "I feel upset when you yell."

Think about times when you've been upset with a friend or family member and complete these sentences:

I feel _____

when you _____.

I feel _____

when you _____.

I feel _____

when you _____.

I feel _____

when you _____.

I feel _____

when you _____.

I feel _____

when you _____.

Listening is a very important part of communicating. How do you feel when somebody isn't listening to you?

_____

_____

_____

_____

How do you know they aren't listening?

_____

_____

_____

_____

When somebody is talking, listen for details and ask questions about those details. What else can you do to listen better to other people?

_____

_____

_____

_____

GROW TOGETHER AS A TEAM

Teams teach you to get along with others. Having a growth mindset will help you focus on what's best for the team instead of how others see you.

Think about when you've been on a team—doing schoolwork, playing a sport, or in some other group. Write about what it was like being part of a team.

_____

_____

_____

_____

_____

How will working on a team now prepare you for a job one day?

_____

_____

_____

_____

_____

"I think, team first.
It allows me to
succeed; it allows
my team to succeed."

—LeBron James, basketball player

Complete the sentences to show how you can put the team first during competitions.

For example, instead of "I want to score the most points," think "I want the team to do well."

Instead of "I want to be the best dancer on the squad," think "I want _____

_____."

Instead of "I want the crowd to cheer for me during my baseball game," think "I want _____

_____."

Instead of "I want to be the best actor in the play," think "I want _____

_____."

Instead of "I want to be the most important person in the group," think "I want _____

_____."

A team is stronger when members have different abilities. Each person brings something different to the group.

What would happen if everyone wanted to do the same job?

_____

_____

_____

_____

_____

What talents could you bring to a team?

_____

_____

_____

_____

_____

Part of contributing to a team involves cheering for your teammates and staying positive.

Write down some positive things you could say if:

Someone puts in extra work. _____

_____

_____

_____

Your team leader is getting frustrated. _____

_____

_____

_____

A teammate has a good idea. _____

_____

_____

_____

CREATE YOUR OWN SUNSHINE FOR SUCCESS

You have the power to create your own happiness even when things aren't great.

Write about a bad day you've had.

_____

_____

_____

What were some good things about that day?

_____

_____

_____

How could focusing on the good things make you have a better day?

_____

_____

_____

"Happiness depends more upon the internal frame of a person's own mind, than on the externals in the world."

—George Washington, first president of the United States

Every day can be a good day if you have the right attitude. Write down four good things you could say about any day (such as animals or sunshine).

_____

_____

_____

_____

You can also daydream about happy things to brighten up a dreary day. Your imagination can be a great escape. Describe your "happy place" or the perfect place to spend time in your mind.

_____

_____

_____

_____

If you could choose anyone (even famous people or book characters), who would you spend time with in your daydreams?

_____

_____

You can always find something positive in any negative situation. When something positive is really hard to find, you can look to the basics, such as having air to breathe, clothes to wear, and food to eat.

Here's an example: I didn't like it when my pencil broke. But my friend was nice and gave me one of theirs.

Now you try.

I didn't like it when _____.

But _____.

I didn't like it when _____.

But _____.

I didn't like it when _____.

But _____.

I didn't like it when _____.

But _____.

I didn't like it when _____.

But _____.

I didn't like it when _____.

But _____.

Don't get sucked into someone else's bad mood. Try to find something positive in any situation so you don't get drawn into negativity.

For example: Today is going to be awful with this rain.

You smile and say, "I love how rain makes the flowers grow."

Now you try!

I hate cleaning my room before a sleepover with friends.

You smile and say, "_____
_____."

This hot weather is making me sweaty and miserable.

You smile and say, "_____
_____."

I ate too much candy and now I'm sick.

You smile and say, "_____
_____."

MINDFULNESS KEEPS YOU IN CONTROL

You have the power to take control of your emotions. With a fixed mindset, you feel like a victim with little control over your emotions. With a growth mindset, you find ways to calm yourself. Mindfulness—being present right now—helps you develop a growth mindset.

Complete this calming activity when your emotions feel too big or out of control.

Right now,

I see _____

and _____.

I hear _____

and _____.

I feel _____

and _____.

I taste _____

and _____.

I smell _____

and _____.

Obsessing over or getting stuck in thoughts about the past or future is distracting. You can stay focused on the present moment by letting things go.

These are worries about the past that I can let go:

These are worries about the future that I can let go:

This is what I can do right now that will help me forget these worries:

Hard times are a normal part of life. They will come and go. Being calm and ready for them will make them a little easier to handle. Write about something you thought was a big deal at the time but now you see it was not so bad.

_____

_____

If you could go back in time, what advice would you give yourself about your hard time?

_____

_____

_____

Knowing that you may have hard times again, write a letter to your future self to let you know that you are ready for those times.

_____

_____

_____

_____

_____

You can make any activity mindful. Think about something you enjoy doing. Notice the details around you and ignore thoughts that aren't related to this activity.

What do I see around me when I do this?

What are the sounds around me when I do this?

What do I smell when I do this?

What do I taste when I do this?

What feelings do I have when I do this?

Positive People
Help You Grow

The people around you can either keep you stuck or help you grow. Carefully choose who you let take up your time.

If you could choose any three positive people in the world to be around, who would they be?

_____

_____

_____

What do you like about them?

_____

_____

_____

What qualities do you share with them?

_____

_____

_____

"If you hang out with chickens, you're going to cluck and if you hang out with eagles, you're going to fly."

—Steve Maraboli, motivational speaker

When you are feeling down, having a positive person around can help you keep going. You can "borrow" their energy. Write about a time when somebody cheered you up and helped you keep going.

_____

_____

_____

How would that time have been different if the person had been negative?

_____

_____

_____

_____

Write about how you will be positive for others when they need it.

_____

_____

_____

_____

Focus on positive conversations and ignore negative ones. Look at the sentences in the negative speech bubbles and find the positive side to them. Write the positive sides in the blank speech bubbles.

Positive friends encourage you to go for your dreams. They don't make fun of them. What dreams do you have that you will share with the positive people in your life?

_____

_____

_____

_____

If you didn't have a positive friend around, what could you say to yourself to keep going for your dreams?

_____

_____

_____

_____

What could you say to somebody who makes fun of your dreams?

_____

_____

_____

_____

CHANGE STARTS WITH THE PERSON IN THE MIRROR

In order to keep growing and learning, you have to be honest with yourself. Look closely at your recent efforts. In the mirror below, list the top three things that take up most of your time, attention, or effort.

What are some other things you would like to see on your list?

_____

_____

_____

_____

_____

_____

What are some things (such as technology or worrying) that you have been giving too much time, effort, or attention to?

_____

_____

_____

_____

_____

_____

_____

Grade the effort that you have been putting into schoolwork this year.

A: I always do my best.

B: I usually do my best.

C: Sometimes I do my best.

D: I don't usually give my best effort.

F: I make very little effort.

_____

What would your teacher say about your schoolwork efforts?

_____

_____

Here's how I plan to improve:

_____

_____

_____

Grade the effort that you have put into being kind to others this year.

A: I go out of my way to be kind to others.

B: I am usually kind to others.

C: Sometimes I am kind.

D: I don't usually think about kindness.

F: I don't think about being kind.

_____

What would your teacher and family say about your efforts to be kind?

_____

_____

Here's how I plan to improve:

_____

_____

_____

Grade the effort that you have put into being neat and organized this year.

A: I go out of my way to be organized.

B: I am usually neat.

C: Sometimes I am organized.

D: I don't usually think about neatness.

F: I don't try to be neat.

_____

What would your teacher and family say about your efforts to be neat and organized?

_____

_____

Here's how I plan to improve:

_____

_____

_____

BE A PROBLEM-SOLVING NINJA

Solving a problem starts with a positive mindset. You have the choice to believe in your ability to solve it.

    Here's a problem I have (or recently had):

_____

_____

_____

_____

    Here's how I feel about my ability to solve my problem: (Circle the spot on the timeline that represents how you feel.)

├───────────────┼───────────────────┼───────────────┤
Confident   Hopeful   Unsure   Hopeless

    How can your attitude affect the amount of effort you put into solving the problem?

_____

_____

_____

_____

"Problems are
only opportunities
in work clothes."

—Henry J. Kaiser, American industrialist

Problems are opportunities to learn.

Instead of "**My problem is** that I'm lonely because my friends moved away," say "**I have the opportunity to learn** how to meet new people."

List a few of your "problems."

My problem is _____.

I have the opportunity to learn _____

_____.

My problem is _____.

I have the opportunity to learn _____

_____.

My problem is _____.

I have the opportunity to learn _____

_____.

How does rewriting your problem as an opportunity make you more confident that you can solve it?

_____

_____

_____

Asking questions and doing research can lead to solutions.

List one of your problems.

_____

Where could you find out more information about it?

_____

_____

_____

Who do you know that may have had this problem before?

_____

_____

_____

What questions could you ask them?

_____

_____

_____

_____

Write down the same problem or a new problem. Brainstorm ideas for solving your problem. Without judging your ideas, write down any ideas that pop into your head.

My problem:

_____

My ideas:

☐ _____

☐ _____

☐ _____

☐ _____

☐ _____

☐ _____

Put a check mark next to the solutions you think would work best.

Choose the best idea from your list and write down three steps toward solving your problem with that solution.

_____

_____

_____

CHOOSE YOUR PATH WITH SMART GOALS

You need goals to succeed, both in your day and in your life. Think about what your day would be like if you didn't make any plans.

What would happen if you didn't make plans or goals for your entire life?

_____

_____

What would happen if you made very specific plans for your life and worked to make them come true?

_____

_____

When making your goals, make sure they are SMART.

S: Specific
M: Measurable
A: Attainable
R: Relevant
T: Timely

"I think goals
should never be easy,
they should force you
to work, even if they
are uncomfortable
at the time."

—Michael Phelps,
Olympic swimming champion

Check the goal that is more **specific** or clear.

- ☐ I want to do better.
- ☐ I want to get higher grades than I have now.

Check the goal that can be **measured**.

- ☐ I want good grades.
- ☐ I want to make all A's.

Create a goal for yourself that is specific and can be measured.

_____

_____

_____

_____

_____

_____

_____

_____

Check the goal that is **attainable**—not too easy or too hard.

- ☐ I want to rule the world.
- ☐ I want to be a successful lawyer.

Check the goal that is **relevant**—tied to something meaningful (and not just silly).

- ☐ I want to help people who are sick.
- ☐ I want to eat a lot of candy.

Create a goal for yourself that is attainable and relevant.

_____

_____

_____

_____

_____

_____

_____

_____

Check the goal that is **timely**—it has a time limit on it so you know when it is completed.

- ☐ I will have good grades one day.
- ☐ I will try out for a sports team by January.

Create a goal for yourself that is timely.

_____

_____

_____

_____

Create a goal that is specific, measurable, attainable, relevant, and timely.

_____

_____

_____

_____

155

NOT "THE END"

Now that you have completed the journal pages, keep this book to remind you of your journey so far. In a few months, go back and work through some of the pages and see if you have the same or different answers. Stay motivated by rechecking your answers at the beginning and end of each school year.

University Growth mindset takes a lot of practice, and you will need to keep working on it. One thing is certain: You will continue to grow and change. Things won't always be perfect, but you will always be able to learn something new from every experience.

Come back to this book, too, when you need a reminder of your strength and awesomeness. Because life gets hard from time to time, I hope you will continue to believe in yourself and use your power to change the way you see things. Continue to create happiness from within and be a positive influence on others.

Before you sign off, answer these last questions.

What are your three favorite ways of practicing a growth mindset?

_____

_____

_____

What have you learned the most about yourself during this process?

_____

_____

_____

_____

_____

_____

_____

_____

Remember, you already have everything it takes to learn, grow, and succeed!

Resources

If you would like more information about growth mindset, check out these books and websites. The books teach valuable lessons about life and the benefits of having a growth mindset through stories. The websites provide more printable resources and lessons to use at home.

Books

Andreae, Giles. *Giraffes Can't Dance*. London: Orchard Books, 2001. This inspirational story shows kids that they are not limited by their current abilities and have the potential to make their dreams come true.

Cook, Julia. *Bubble Gum Brain*. Chattanooga, TN: National Center for Youth Issues, 2017. In this book, kids are encouraged to have a growth mindset and enjoy the journey of learning from mistakes.

Cornwall, Gaia. *Jabari Jumps*. Somerville, MA: Candlewick, 2017. An encouraging book that demonstrates the power of overcoming fears and trying new things.

Deak, JoAnn. *Your Fantastic Elastic Brain: Stretch It, Shape It*. Naperville, IL: Little Pickle Press, 2010. This book takes a relatable look at how the brain works and how having a growth mindset will take you far in life.

Pett, Mark, and Gary Rubinstein. *The Girl Who Never Made Mistakes*. Naperville, IL: Sourcebooks, 2011. This is a fun and instructive book on becoming comfortable with making mistakes and letting go of perfection because it gets in the way of creativity.

Reynolds, Peter H. *The Dot*. Somerville, MA: Candlewick, 2003. This book encourages kids to find their bravery and take that first step when something is holding them back.

Saltzberg, Barney. *Beautiful Oops*. New York, NY: Workman Publishing, 2010. A beautiful interactive pop-up book that celebrates the beauty of turning mistakes into creative wonders.

Websites

Mindsetkit.org is filled with free online resources for teaching growth mindset to kids.

Mindsetworks.com is dedicated to bringing the power of growth mindset to schools and families through curriculum and easy to understand tips.

MindUP.org has a research-based social emotional curriculum for educators and tips for parents to implement mindful activities at home.

Thenedshow.com/mindset-lesson-plans has a wonderful library of free printable resources for parents and educators to teach growth mindset through a variety of engaging activities.

References

Amit Ray. https://amitray.com/mindfulness
-growth-mindset-neuroscience

Bits of Positivity. https://bitsofpositivity.com/best
-growth-mindset-quotes-for-kids-and-adults

Everyday Power Blog. https://everydaypowerblog
.com/self-reflection-quotes

Examined Existence. https://examinedexistence
.com/how-long-does-it-take-for-something-to
-become-a-habit

Brain Plasticity. http://faculty.washington.edu
/chudler/plast.html

Acknowledgments

I would like to thank Susan, Katie, and the Callisto Media team for choosing me to author this book on a topic that I feel so passionate about. It was an amazing journey and I appreciate the guidance and support.

Thank you to my husband, Sam, for always believing in me and taking on all the chores while I was wrapped up in writing. A special thanks to my daughter, Emma, for reading through the prompts to see if they were kid friendly. Thanks to my amazingly smart boys, Denver and Nic, who gave valuable feedback when I needed to brainstorm ideas for the journal.

Love and thanks to my parents, Nancy and Benny, in heaven who loved me unconditionally and taught me to believe in myself.

About the Author

BRANDY THOMPSON is an education curriculum writer in Germantown, Tennessee. She is the author and creator of TheCounselingTeacher.com where she shows school counselors how to reach students through games, crafts, and interactive lessons. She obtained a bachelor of arts degree in psychology at the University of Memphis, a master of teaching degree at Freed Hardeman in Henderson, Tennessee, and a master of education in school counseling from the University of Tennessee at Martin. She began her education career in 2007 teaching 2nd, 4th, and 8th grades. Discovering her passion for the social-emotional needs of children, she transitioned into school counseling in 2014. In 2016, her school counseling program was awarded the Recognized ASCA Model Program (RAMP) award from the American School Counseling Association.